MY FIRST SPORTS

Soccer

by Anne Wendorff

BLASTOFF! READERS
4

BELLWETHER MEDIA • MINNEAPOLIS, MN

Note to Librarians, Teachers, and Parents:

Blastoff! Readers are carefully developed by literacy experts and combine standards-based content with developmentally appropriate text.

Level 1 provides the most support through repetition of high-frequency words, light text, predictable sentence patterns, and strong visual support.

Level 2 offers early readers a bit more challenge through varied simple sentences, increased text load, and less repetition of high-frequency words.

Level 3 advances early-fluent readers toward fluency through increased text and concept load, less reliance on visuals, longer sentences, and more literary language.

Level 4 builds reading stamina by providing more text per page, increased use of punctuation, greater variation in sentence patterns, and increasingly challenging vocabulary.

Level 5 encourages children to move from "learning to read" to "reading to learn" by providing even more text, varied writing styles, and less familiar topics.

Whichever book is right for your reader, Blastoff! Readers are the perfect books to build confidence and encourage a love of reading that will last a lifetime!

This edition first published in 2010 by Bellwether Media, Inc.

No part of this publication may be reproduced in whole or in part without written permission of the publisher. For information regarding permission, write to Bellwether Media, Inc., Attention: Permissions Department, 5357 Penn Avenue South, Minneapolis, MN 55419.

Library of Congress Cataloging-in-Publication Data
Wendorff, Anne.
  Soccer / by Anne Wendorff.
    p. cm. – (Blastoff! readers. My first sports)
  Includes bibliographical references and index.
  Summary: "Simple text and full color photographs introduce beginning readers to the sport of soccer. Developed by literacy experts for students in grades two through five"–Provided by publisher.
  ISBN 978-1-60014-329-8 (hardcover : alk. paper)   4335   0683   11/10
  1. Soccer–Juvenile literature. I. Title.

GV943.25.W46 2009
796.334–dc22
                           2009008183

Text copyright © 2010 by Bellwether Media, Inc.
Printed in the United States of America, North Mankato, MN.

021510   1159

Contents

What Is Soccer?

Soccer is a team sport where players try to score goals to win a game. It is considered to be the most popular sport in the world. There are several soccer leagues in many different countries.

fun fact

Soccer is called "football" in most countries. It is called "football" because players kick the soccer ball with their feet.

Soccer was first played in England in the 1800s. When schools began forming soccer teams, each team played soccer differently. To play each other, the teams needed to agree on a set of rules.

A group of soccer teams met and formed the Football Association (FA) in England. The FA wrote down the official rules of soccer. This group is still in charge of soccer in England today.

The Basic Rules of Soccer

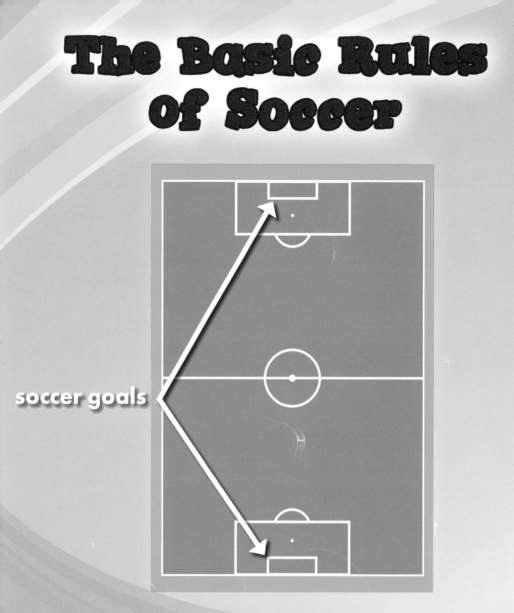

soccer goals

A soccer game is called a **match**. A soccer match is played on a field. The field is 100 yards (91 meters) long and 60 yards (55 meters) wide. A big net called a **soccer goal** is set up at each end of the field.

Players score goals by hitting the soccer ball into the other team's soccer goal. A team must work together in order to score. They must run, pass, and kick their way to victory. The team with the most goals at the end of the match wins.

Each team has 11 players on the field during a match. Each player has a position. The four positions are **forward**, **midfielder**, **fullback**, and **goalie**.

Forwards score points. Midfielders help score points and defend their soccer goal. Fullbacks stop the other team from scoring. Goalies stop the ball from entering the soccer goals.

Players must kick the ball in soccer.
They kick it to pass to teammates close to
them or far down the field. Forwards and
midfielders try to kick the ball hard and fast
to get it past the goalie!

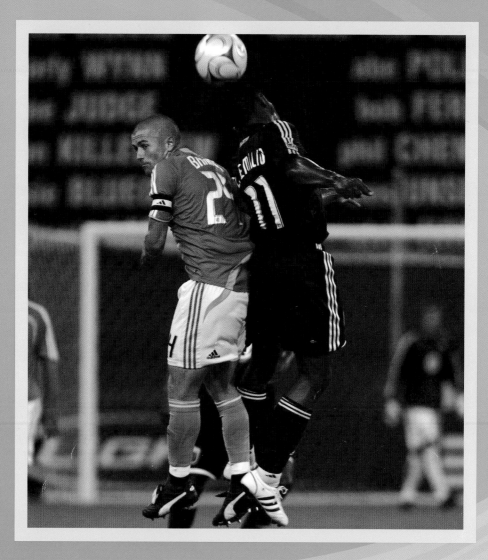

Players can also hit the ball with their chests or heads. Goalies are the only players allowed to touch the ball with their hands. Other players receive a **penalty** if they use their hands during the match.

Referees carry a yellow card and a red card. Referees pull out the cards when they give a player a penalty. Players are given a yellow card for minor penalties. Players are given a red card for major penalties. A player who is given a red card is kicked out of the match.

fun fact

If a player receives a penalty, the other team gets a free kick. During a free kick, the ball is kicked from the spot on the field where the penalty took place.

Soccer Equipment

Soccer players wear equipment to keep them safe. **Shin guards** protect their legs. Soccer goalies wear gloves to protect their hands. Gloves also help goalies catch and hold on to the ball.

Players also wear shoes with metal or plastic spikes called **cleats**. Cleats help players run and stop quickly without sliding on the field.

Soccer Today

Soccer is one of the world's most popular sports. The sport's biggest event is called the **World Cup**. Every four years, teams from all over the world compete in this tournament.

The soccer team from Brazil holds the record for the most World Cup titles. They have won five times.

Soccer is the fastest-growing sport in America. The United States' professional soccer league is called Major League Soccer (MLS). There are 16 teams in the league. The MLS hosts day camps to help young players become tomorrow's soccer stars.

Glossary

cleats—the metal or plastic spikes on the bottom of shoes; cleats help a soccer player run on a field.

forward—a soccer position; a forward's job is to score goals.

fullback—a soccer position; a fullback's job is to stop the other team from scoring.

goalie—a soccer position; the goalie's job is to stop the ball from entering the goal.

match—a soccer game

midfielder—a soccer position; a midfielder's job is to help both forwards and fullbacks.

penalty—a punishment for not following game rules

referee—a person who makes sure players follow game rules

shin guards—the soft pads tied to a soccer player's legs for protection

soccer goal—a large net; players must hit the ball into the net to score a goal.

World Cup—the biggest international soccer tournament

To Learn More

AT THE LIBRARY

Christopher, Matt and Stephanie Peters. *Soccer Hero*. New York, N.Y.: Little Brown Books for Young Readers, 2007.

Gibbons, Gail. *My Soccer Book*. New York, N.Y.: HarperCollins, 2000.

Hornby, Hugh. *Soccer*. New York, N.Y.: DK Publishing, 2008.

ON THE WEB

Learning more about soccer is as easy as 1, 2, 3.

1. Go to www.factsurfer.com.

2. Enter "soccer" into the search box.

3. Click the "Surf" button and you will see a list of related Web sites.

With factsurfer.com, finding more information is just a click away.

Index